CITY TREES

THE trees along this city street,

   Save for the traffic and the trains,

Would make a sound as thin and sweet

   As trees in country lanes.

And people standing in their shade

   Out of a shower, undoubtedly

Would hear such music as is made

   Upon a country tree.

Oh, little leaves that are so dumb

   Against the shrieking city air,

I watch you when the wind has come,—

   I know what sound is there.

THE BLUE-FLAG IN THE BOG

God had called us, and we came;
  Our loved Earth to ashes left;
Heaven was a neighbor's house,
  Open flung to us, bereft.

Gay the lights of Heaven showed,
  And 'twas God who walked ahead;
Yet I wept along the road,
  Wanting my own house instead.

Wept unseen, unheeded cried,
  "All you things my eyes have kissed,
Fare you well! We meet no more,
  Lovely, lovely tattered mist!

4

Weary wings that rise and fall
   All day long above the fire!"—
Red with heat was every wall,
   Rough with heat was every wire—

"Fare you well, you little winds
   That the flying embers chase!
Fare you well, you shuddering day,
   With your hands before your face!

And, ah, blackened by strange blight,
   Or to a false sun unfurled,
Now forevermore goodbye,
   All the gardens in the world!

On the windless hills of Heaven,
   That I have no wish to see,

5

White, eternal lilies stand,
  By a lake of ebony.

But the Earth forevermore
  Is a place where nothing grows,—
Dawn will come, and no bud break;
  Evening, and no blossom close.

Spring will come, and wander slow
  Over an indifferent land,
Stand beside an empty creek,
  Hold a dead seed in her hand."

God had called us, and we came,
  But the blessed road I trod
Was a bitter road to me,
  And at heart I questioned God.

6

"Though in Heaven," I said, "be all
   That the heart would most desire,
Held Earth naught save souls of sinners
   Worth the saving from a fire?

Withered grass,—the wasted growing!
   Aimless ache of laden boughs!"
Little things God had forgotten
   Called me, from my burning house.

"Though in Heaven," I said, "be all
   That the eye could ask to see,
All the things I ever knew
   Are this blaze in back of me."

"Though in Heaven," I said, "be all
   That the ear could think to lack,

All the things I ever knew

    Are this roaring at my back."

It was God who walked ahead,

    Like a shepherd to the fold;

In his footsteps fared the weak,

    And the weary and the old,

Glad enough of gladness over,

    Ready for the peace to be,—

But a thing God had forgotten

    Was the growing bones of me.

And I drew a bit apart,

    And I lagged a bit behind,

And I thought on Peace Eternal,

    Lest He look into my mind;

And I gazed upon the sky,

   And I thought of Heavenly Rest,—

And I slipped away like water

   Through the fingers of the blest!

All their eyes were fixed on Glory,

   Not a glance brushed over me;

"Alleluia!   Alleluia!"

   Up the road,--and I was free.

And my heart rose like a freshet,

   And it swept me on before,

Giddy as a whirling stick,

   Till I felt the earth once more.

All the Earth was charred and black,

   Fire had swept from pole to pole;

9

And the bottom of the sea
  Was as brittle as a bowl;

And the timbered mountain-top
  Was as naked as a skull,—
Nothing left, nothing left,
  Of the Earth so beautiful!

"Earth," I said, "how can I leave you?"
  "You are all I have," I said;
"What is left to take my mind up,
  Living always, and you dead?"

"Speak!" I said, "Oh, tell me something!
  Make a sign that I can see!
For a keepsake! To keep always!
  Quick!—before God misses me!"

And I listened for a voice;—

  But my heart was all I heard;

Not a screech-owl, not a loon,

  Not a tree-toad said a word.

And I waited for a sign;—

  Coals and cinders, nothing more;

And a little cloud of smoke

  Floating on a valley floor.

And I peered into the smoke

  Till it rotted, like a fog:—

There, encompassed round by fire,

  Stood a blue-flag in a bog!

Little flames came wading out,

  Straining, straining towards its stem,

But it was so blue and tall

    That it scorned to think of them!

Red and thirsty were their tongues,

    As the tongues of wolves must be,

But it was so blue and tall—

    Oh, I laughed, I cried, to see!

All my heart became a tear,

    All my soul became a tower,

Never loved I anything

    As I loved that tall blue flower!

It was all the little boats

    That had ever sailed the sea,

It was all the little books

    That had gone to school with me;

On its roots like iron claws
  Rearing up so blue and tall,—
It was all the gallant Earth
  With its back against a wall!

In a breath, ere I had breathed,—
  Oh, I laughed, I cried, to see!—
I was kneeling at its side,
  And it leaned its head on me!

Crumbling stones and sliding sand
  Is the road to Heaven now;
Icy at my straining knees
  Drags the awful under-tow;

Soon but stepping-stones of dust
  Will the road to Heaven be,—

Father, Son and Holy Ghost,
  Reach a hand and rescue me!

"There—there, my blue-flag flower;
  Hush—hush—go to sleep;
That is only God you hear,
  Counting up His folded sheep!

Lullabye—lullabye—
  That is only God that calls,
Missing me, seeking me,
  Ere the road to nothing falls!

He will set His mighty feet
  Firmly on the sliding sand;
Like a little frightened bird
  I will creep into His hand;

14

I will tell Him all my grief,

   I will tell Him all my sin;

He will give me half His robe

   For a cloak to wrap you in.

Lullabye—lullabye—"

   Rocks the burnt-out planet free!—

Father, Son and Holy Ghost,

   Reach a hand and rescue me!

Ah, the voice of love at last!

   Lo, at last the face of light!

And the whole of His white robe

   For a cloak against the night!

And upon my heart asleep

   All the things I ever knew!—

"Holds Heaven not some cranny, Lord,
For a flower so tall and blue?"

All's well and all's well!
Gay the lights of Heaven show!
In some moist and Heavenly place
We will set it out to grow.

JOURNEY

Ah, could I lay me down in this long grass
And close my eyes, and let the quiet wind
Blow over me,—I am so tired, so tired
Of passing pleasant places! All my life,
Following Care along the dusty road,
Have I looked back at loveliness and sighed;
Yet at my hand an unrelenting hand
Tugged ever, and I passed. All my life long
Over my shoulder have I looked at peace;
And now I fain would lie in this long grass
And close my eyes.

        Yet onward!

             Cat-birds call

JOURNEY

Through the long afternoon, and creeks at dusk
Are guttural. Whip-poor-wills wake and cry,
Drawing the twilight close about their throats.
Only my heart makes answer. Eager vines
Go up the rocks and wait; flushed apple-trees
Pause in their dance and break the ring for me;
Dim, shady wood-roads, redolent of fern
And bayberry, that through sweet bevies thread
Of round-faced roses, pink and petulant,
Look back and beckon ere they disappear.
Only my heart, only my heart responds.
Yet, ah, my path is sweet on either side
All through the dragging day,—sharp underfoot,
And hot, and like dead mist the dry dust hangs—
But far, oh, far as passionate eye can reach,
And long, ah, long as rapturous eye can cling,

JOURNEY

The world is mine: blue hill, still silver lake,

Broad field, bright flower, and the long white road

A gateless garden, and an open path:

My feet to follow, and my heart to hold.

EEL-GRASS

No matter what I say,
   All that I really love
Is the rain that flattens on the bay,
   And the eel-grass in the cove;
The jingle-shells that lie and bleach
   At the tide-line, and the trace
Of higher tides along the beach:
   Nothing in this place.

ELEGY BEFORE DEATH

THERE will be rose and rhododendron
  When you are dead and under ground;
Still will be heard from white syringas
  Heavy with bees, a sunny sound;

Still will the tamaracks be raining
  After the rain has ceased, and still
Will there be robins in the stubble,
  Brown sheep upon the warm green hill.

Spring will not ail nor autumn falter;
  Nothing will know that you are gone,
Saving alone some sullen plough-land
  None but yourself sets foot upon;

Saving the may-weed and the pig-weed
  Nothing will know that you are dead,—
These, and perhaps a useless wagon
  Standing beside some tumbled shed.

Oh, there will pass with your great passing
  Little of beauty not your own,—
Only the light from common water,
  Only the grace from simple stone!

THE BEAN-STALK

Ho, Giant! This is I!

I have built me a bean-stalk into your sky!

La,—but it's lovely, up so high!

This is how I came,—I put

Here my knee, there my foot,

Up and up, from shoot to shoot—

And the blessèd bean-stalk thinning

Like the mischief all the time,

Till it took me rocking, spinning,

In a dizzy, sunny circle,

Making angles with the root,

Far and out above the cackle

Of the city I was born in,

Till the little dirty city

In the light so sheer and sunny

Shone as dazzling bright and pretty

As the money that you find

In a dream of finding money—

What a wind!   What a morning!—

Till the tiny, shiny city,

When I shot a glance below,

Shaken with a giddy laughter,

Sick and blissfully afraid,

Was a dew-drop on a blade,

And a pair of moments after

Was the whirling guess I made,—

And the wind was like a whip

24

THE BEAN-STALK

Cracking past my icy ears,

And my hair stood out behind,

And my eyes were full of tears,

Wide-open and cold,

More tears than they could hold,

The wind was blowing so,

And my teeth were in a row,

Dry and grinning,

And I felt my foot slip,

And I scratched the wind and whined,

And I clutched the stalk and jabbered,

With my eyes shut blind,—

What a wind! What a wind!

Your broad sky, Giant,

Is the shelf of a cupboard;

THE BEAN-STALK

I make bean-stalks, I'm

A builder, like yourself,

But bean-stalks is my trade,

I couldn't make a shelf,

Don't know how they're made,

Now, a bean-stalk is more pliant—

La, what a climb!

WEEDS

WHITE with daisies and red with sorrel
　And empty, empty under the sky!—
Life is a quest and love a quarrel—
　Here is a place for me to lie.

Daisies spring from damnèd seeds,
　And this red fire that here I see
Is a worthless crop of crimson weeds,
　Cursed by farmers thriftily.

But here, unhated for an hour,
　The sorrel runs in ragged flame,
The daisy stands, a bastard flower,
　Like flowers that bear an honest name.

27

WEEDS

And here a while, where no wind brings

The baying of a pack athirst,

May sleep the sleep of blessèd things

The blood too bright, the brow accurst.

PASSER MORTUUS EST

DEATH devours all lovely things;
　　Lesbia with her sparrow
Shares the darkness,—presently
　　Every bed is narrow

Unremembered as old rain
　　Dries the sheer libation,
And the little petulant hand
　　Is an annotation.

After all, my erstwhile dear,
　　My no longer cherished,
Need we say it was not love,
　　Now that love is perished?

29

PASTORAL

IF it were only still!—
With far away the shrill
Crying of a cock;
Or the shaken bell
From a cow's throat
Moving through the bushes;
Or the soft shock
Of wizened apples falling
From an old tree
In a forgotten orchard
Upon the hilly rock!

Oh, grey hill,
Where the grazing herd

PASTORAL

Licks the purple blossom,

Crops the spiky weed!

Oh, stony pasture,

Where the tall mullein

Stands up so sturdy

On its little seed!

ASSAULT

I

I HAD forgotten how the frogs must sound

After a year of silence, else I think

I should not so have ventured forth alone

At dusk upon this unfrequented road.

II

I am waylaid by Beauty.   Who will walk

Between me and the crying of the frogs?

Oh, savage Beauty, suffer me to pass,

That am a timid woman, on her way

From one house to another!

32

TRAVEL

THE railroad track is miles away,

    And the day is loud with voices speaking,

Yet there isn't a train goes by all day

    But I hear its whistle shrieking.

All night there isn't a train goes by,

    Though the night is still for sleep and dreaming,

But I see its cinders red on the sky,

    And hear its engine steaming.

My heart is warm with the friends I make,

    And better friends I'll not be knowing,

Yet there isn't a train I wouldn't take,

    No matter where it's going.

LOW-TIDE

THESE wet rocks where the tide has been,
  Barnacled white and weeded brown
And slimed beneath to a beautiful green,
  These wet rocks where the tide went down
Will show again when the tide is high
  Faint and perilous, far from shore,
No place to dream, but a place to die,—
  The bottom of the sea once more.
There was a child that wandered through
  A giant's empty house all day,—
House full of wonderful things and new,
  But no fit place for a child to play.

SONG OF A SECOND APRIL

APRIL this year, not otherwise
   Than April of a year ago,
Is full of whispers, full of sighs,
   Of dazzling mud and dingy snow;
   Hepaticas that pleased you so
Are here again, and butterflies.

There rings a hammering all day,
   And shingles lie about the doors;
In orchards near and far away
   The grey wood-pecker taps and bores;
   And men are merry at their chores,
And children earnest at their play.

35

The larger streams run still and deep,

   Noisy and swift the small brooks run

Among the mullein stalks the sheep

   Go up the hillside in the sun,

   Pensively,—only you are gone,

You that alone I cared to keep.

ROSEMARY

FOR the sake of some things
   That be now no more
I will strew rushes
   On my chamber-floor,
I will plant bergamot
   At my kitchen-door.

For the sake of dim things
   That were once so plain
I will set a barrel
   Out to catch the rain,
I will hang an iron pot
   On an iron crane.

37

Many things be dead and gone

    That were brave and gay;

For the sake of these things

    I will learn to say,

"An it please you, gentle sirs,"

    "Alack!" and "Well-a-day!"

THE POET AND HIS BOOK

Down, you mongrel, Death!
Back into your kennel!
I have stolen breath
In a stalk of fennel!
You shall scratch and you shall whine
Many a night, and you shall worry
Many a bone, before you bury
One sweet bone of mine!

When shall I be dead?
  When my flesh is withered,
And above my head
  Yellow pollen gathered

39

All the empty afternoon?

  When sweet lovers pause and wonder

  Who am I that lie thereunder,

Hidden from the moon?

This my personal death?—

  That my lungs be failing

To inhale the breath

  Others are exhaling?

This my subtle spirit's end?—

  Ah, when the thawed winter splashes

  Over these chance dust and ashes,

Weep not me, my friend!

Me, by no means dead

  In that hour, but surely

When this book, unread,

Rots to earth obscurely,

And no more to any breast,

    Close against the clamorous swelling

    Of the thing there is no telling,

Are these pages pressed!

When this book is mould,

    And a book of many

Waiting to be sold

    For a casual penny,

In a little open case,

    In a street unclean and cluttered,

    Where a heavy mud is spattered

From the passing drays,

Stranger, pause and look;

    From the dust of ages

Lift this little book,

   Turn the tattered pages,

Read me, do not let me die!

   Search the fading letters, finding

   Steadfast in the broken binding

All that once was I!

When these veins are weeds,

   When these hollowed sockets

Watch the rooty seeds

   Bursting down like rockets,

And surmise the spring again,

   Or, remote in that black cupboard,

   Watch the pink worms writhing upward

At the smell of rain,

Boys and girls that lie

Whispering in the hedges,

Do not let me die,

Mix me with your pledges;

Boys and girls that slowly walk

In the woods, and weep, and quarrel,

Staring past the pink wild laurel,

Mix me with your talk,

Do not let me die!

Farmers at your raking,

When the sun is high,

While the hay is making,

When, along the stubble strewn,

Withering on their stalks uneaten,

Strawberries turn dark and sweeten

In the lapse of noon;

43

Shepherds on the hills,

   In the pastures, drowsing

To the tinkling bells

   Of the brown sheep browsing;

Sailors crying through the storm;

   Scholars at your study; hunters

   Lost amid the whirling winter's

Whiteness uniform;

Men that long for sleep;

   Men that wake and revel;—

If an old song leap

   To your senses' level

At such moments, may it be

   Sometimes, though a moment only,

   Some forgotten, quaint and homely

Vehicle of me!

Women at your toil,

 Women at your leisure

Till the kettle boil,

 Snatch of me your pleasure,

Where the broom-straw marks the leaf;

 Women quiet with your weeping

 Lest you wake a workman sleeping,

Mix me with your grief!

Boys and girls that steal

 From the shocking laughter

Of the old, to kneel

 By a dripping rafter

Under the discolored eaves,

 Out of trunks with hingeless covers

 Lifting tales of saints and lovers,

Travelers, goblins, thieves,

Suns that shine by night,
    Mountains made from valleys,—
Bear me to the light,
    Flat upon your bellies
By the webby window lie,
    Where the little flies are crawling,—
    Read me, margin me with scrawling,
Do not let me die!

Sexton, ply your trade!
    In a shower of gravel
Stamp upon your spade!
    Many a rose shall ravel,
Many a metal wreath shall rust
    In the rain, and I go singing
    Through the lots where you are flinging
Yellow clay on dust!

ALMS

My heart is what it was before,

    A house where people come and go;

But it is winter with your love,

    The sashes are beset with snow.

I light the lamp and lay the cloth,

    I blow the coals to blaze again;

But it is winter with your love,

    The frost is thick upon the pane.

I know a winter when it comes:

    The leaves are listless on the boughs;

I watched your love a little while,

    And brought my plants into the house.

I water them and turn them south,

    I snap the dead brown from the stem;

But it is winter with your love,—

    I only tend and water them.

There was a time I stood and watched

    The small, ill-natured sparrows' fray;

I loved the beggar that I fed,

    I cared for what he had to say,

I stood and watched him out of sight;

    Today I reach around the door

And set a bowl upon the step;

    My heart is what it was before,

But it is winter with your love;

    I scatter crumbs upon the sill,

And close the window,—and the birds

    May take or leave them, as they will.

INLAND

PEOPLE that build their houses inland,
  People that buy a plot of ground
Shaped like a house, and build a house there,
  Far from the sea-board, far from the sound

Of water sucking the hollow ledges,
  Tons of water striking the shore,—
What do they long for, as I long for
  One salt smell of the sea once more?

People the waves have not awakened,
  Spanking the boats at the harbor's head,
What do they long for, as I long for,—
  Starting up in my inland bed,

49

INLAND

Beating the narrow walls, and finding

Neither a window nor a door,

Screaming to God for death by drowning,—

One salt taste of the sea once more?

TO A POET THAT DIED YOUNG

Minstrel, what have you to do
With this man that, after you,
Sharing not your happy fate,
Sat as England's Laureate?
Vainly, in these iron days,
Strives the poet in your praise,
Minstrel, by whose singing side
Beauty walked, until you died.

Still, though none should hark again,
Drones the blue-fly in the pane,
Thickly crusts the blackest moss,
Blows the rose its musk across,

51

Floats the boat that is forgot
None the less to Camelot.

Many a bard's untimely death
Lends unto his verses breath;
Here's a song was never sung:
Growing old is dying young.
Minstrel, what is this to you:
That a man you never knew,
When your grave was far and green,
Sat and gossipped with a queen?

Thalia knows how rare a thing
Is it, to grow old and sing;
When a brown and tepid tide
Closes in on every side.
Who shall say if Shelley's gold
Had withstood it to grow old?

WRAITH

"Thin Rain, whom are you haunting,
  That you haunt my door?"
—Surely it is not I she's wanting;
  Someone living here before—
"Nobody's in the house but me:
You may come in if you like and see."

Thin as thread, with exquisite fingers,—
  Have you seen her, any of you?—
Grey shawl, and leaning on the wind,
  And the garden showing through?

Glimmering eyes,—and silent, mostly,
  Sort of a whisper, sort of a purr,

Asking something, asking it over,

    If you get a sound from her.—

Ever see her, any of you?—

    Strangest thing I've ever known,—

Every night since I moved in,

    And I came to be alone.

"Thin Rain, hush with your knocking!

    You may not come in!

This is I that you hear rocking;

    Nobody's with me, nor has been!"

Curious, how she tried the window,—

    Odd, the way she tries the door,—

Wonder just what sort of people

    Could have had this house before . . .

54

EBB

I KNOW what my heart is like
   Since your love died:
It is like a hollow ledge
Holding a little pool
   Left there by the tide,
   A little tepid pool,
Drying inward from the edge.

ELAINE

Oh, come again to Astolat!
  I will not ask you to be kind.
And you may go when you will go,
  And I will stay behind.

I will not say how dear you are,
  Or ask you if you hold me dear,
Or trouble you with things for you
  The way I did last year.

So still the orchard, Lancelot,
  So very still the lake shall be,
You could not guess—though you should
    guess—
  What is become of me.

56

ELAINE

So wide shall be the garden-walk,

   The garden-seat so very wide,

You needs must think—if you should

     think—

   The lily maid had died.

Save that, a little way away,

   I'd watch you for a little while,

To see you speak, the way you speak,

   And smile,—if you should smile.

BURIAL

MINE is a body that should die at sea!
  And have for a grave, instead of a grave
Six feet deep and the length of me,
  All the water that is under the wave!

And terrible fishes to seize my flesh,
  Such as a living man might fear,
And eat me while I am firm and fresh,—
  Not wait till I've been dead for a year!

MARIPOSA

BUTTERFLIES are white and blue
In this field we wander through.
Suffer me to take your hand.
Death comes in a day or two.

All the things we ever knew
Will be ashes in that hour,
Mark the transient butterfly,
How he hangs upon the flower.

Suffer me to take your hand.
Suffer me to cherish you
Till the dawn is in the sky.
Whether I be false or true,
Death comes in a day or two.

THE LITTLE HILL

Oh, here the air is sweet and still,

And soft's the grass to lie on;

And far away's the little hill

They took for Christ to die on.

And there's a hill across the brook,

And down the brook's another;

But, oh, the little hill they took,—

I think I am its mother!

The moon that saw Gethsemane,

I watch it rise and set;

It has so many things to see,

They help it to forget.

60

THE LITTLE HILL

But little hills that sit at home
So many hundred years,
Remember Greece, remember Rome,
Remember Mary's tears.

And far away in Palestine,
Sadder than any other,
Grieves still the hill that I call mine,—
I think I am its mother!

DOUBT NO MORE THAT OBERON

Doubt no more that Oberon—
Never doubt that Pan
Lived, and played a reed, and ran
After nymphs in a dark forest,
In the merry, credulous days,—
Lived, and led a fairy band
Over the indulgent land!
Ah, for in this dourest, sorest
Age man's eye has looked upon,
Death to fauns and death to fays,
Still the dog-wood dares to raise—
Healthy tree, with trunk and root—

Ivory bowls that bear no fruit,

And the starlings and the jays—

Birds that cannot even sing—

Dare to come again in spring!

LAMENT

LISTEN, children:

Your father is dead.

From his old coats

I'll make you little jackets;

I'll make you little trousers

From his old pants.

There'll be in his pockets

Things he used to put there,

Keys and pennies

Covered with tobacco;

Dan shall have the pennies

To save in his bank;

Anne shall have the keys

To make a pretty noise with.

Life must go on,

And the dead be forgotten;

Life must go on,

Though good men die;

Anne, eat your breakfast;

Dan, take your medicine;

Life must go on;

I forget just why.

EXILED

SEARCHING my heart for its true sorrow,
  This is the thing I find to be:
That I am weary of words and people,
  Sick of the city, wanting the sea;

Wanting the sticky, salty sweetness
  Of the strong wind and shattered spray;
Wanting the loud sound and the soft sound
  Of the big surf that breaks all day.

Always before about my dooryard,
  Marking the reach of the winter sea,
Rooted in sand and dragging drift-wood,
  Straggled the purple wild sweet-pea;

EXILED

Always I climbed the wave at morning,
  Shook the sand from my shoes at night,
That now am caught beneath great buildings,
  Stricken with noise, confused with light.

If I could hear the green piles groaning
  Under the windy wooden piers,
See once again the bobbing barrels,
  And the black sticks that fence the weirs.

If I could see the weedy mussels
  Crusting the wrecked and rotting hulls,
Hear once again the hungry crying
  Overhead, of the wheeling gulls,

Feel once again the shanty straining
  Under the turning of the tide,

Fear once again the rising freshet,
  Dread the bell in the fog outside,—

I should be happy,—that was happy
  All day long on the coast of Maine!
I have a need to hold and handle
  Shells and anchors and ships again!

I should be happy, that am happy
  Never at all since I came here.
I am too long away from water.
  I have a need of water near.

THE DEATH OF AUTUMN

WHEN reeds are dead and a straw to thatch the
    marshes,
And feathered pampas-grass rides into the wind
Like agèd warriors westward, tragic, thinned
Of half their tribe, and over the flattened rushes,
Stripped of its secret, open, stark and bleak,
Blackens afar the half-forgotten creek,—
Then leans on me the weight of the year, and
    crushes
My heart. I know that Beauty must ail and die,
And will be born again,—but ah, to see
Beauty stiffened, staring up at the sky!
Oh, Autumn! Autumn!—What is the Spring
    to me?

ODE TO SILENCE

Aye, but she?

Your other sister and my other soul

Grave Silence, lovelier

Than the three loveliest maidens, what of her?

Clio, not you,

Not you, Calliope,

Nor all your wanton line,

Not Beauty's perfect self shall comfort me

For Silence once departed,

For her the cool-tongued, her the tranquil-
hearted,

Whom evermore I follow wistfully,

ODE TO SILENCE

Wandering Heaven and Earth and Hell and the
  four seasons through;
Thalia, not you,
Not you, Melpomene,
Not your incomparable feet, O thin Terpsichore,
I seek in this great hall,
But one more pale, more pensive, most beloved
  of you all.

I seek her from afar.
I come from temples where her altars are,
From groves that bear her name,
Noisy with stricken victims now and sacrificial
  flame,
And cymbals struck on high and strident faces
Obstreperous in her praise

They neither love nor know,

A goddess of gone days,

Departed long ago,

Abandoning the invaded shrines and fanes

Of her old sanctuary,

A deity obscure and legendary,

Of whom there now remains,

For sages to decipher and priests to garble,

Only and for a little while her letters wedged
in marble,

Which even now, behold, the friendly mumbling
rain erases,

And the inarticulate snow,

Leaving at last of her least signs and traces

None whatsoever, nor whither she is vanished
from these places.

"She will love well," I said,

"If love be of that heart inhabiter,

The flowers of the dead;

The red anemone that with no sound

Moves in the wind, and from another wound

That sprang, the heavily-sweet blue hyacinth,

That blossoms underground,

And sallow poppies, will be dear to her.

And will not Silence know

In the black shade of what obsidian steep

Stiffens the white narcissus numb with sleep?

(Seed which Demeter's daughter bore from home

Uptorn by desperate fingers long ago,

Reluctant even as she,

Undone Persephone,

And even as she set out again to grow

73

In twilight, in perdition's lean and inauspicious
    loam).

She will love well," I said,

"The flowers of the dead;

Where dark Persephone the winter round,

Uncomforted for home, uncomforted,

Lacking a sunny southern slope in northern Sicily,

With sullen pupils focussed on a dream,

Stares on the stagnant stream

That moats the unequivocable battlements of
    Hell,

There, there will she be found,

She that is Beauty veiled from men and Music in
    a swound."

"I long for Silence as they long for breath

Whose helpless nostrils drink the bitter sea;

What thing can be

So stout, what so redoubtable, in Death

What fury, what considerable rage, if only she,

Upon whose icy breast,

Unquestioned, uncaressed,

One time I lay,

And whom always I lack,

Even to this day,

Being by no means from that frigid bosom weaned

away,

If only she therewith be given me back?"

I sought her down that dolorous labyrinth,

Wherein no shaft of sunlight ever fell,

And in among the bloodless everywhere

I sought her, but the air,

Breathed many times and spent,

Was fretful with a whispering discontent,

And questioning me, importuning me to tell

Some slightest tidings of the light of day they know

no more,

Plucking my sleeve, the eager shades were with me

where I went.

I paused at every grievous door,

And harked a moment, holding up my hand,—

and for a space

A hush was on them, while they watched my

face;

And then they fell a-whispering as before;

So that I smiled at them and left them, seeing she

was not there.

76

I sought her, too,

Among the upper gods, although I knew

She was not like to be where feasting is,

Nor near to Heaven's lord,

Being a thing abhorred

And shunned of him, although a child of his,

(Not yours, not yours; to you she owes not
    breath,

Mother of Song, being sown of Zeus upon a dream
    of Death).

Fearing to pass unvisited some place

And later learn, too late, how all the while,

With her still face,

She had been standing there and seen me pass, with-
    out a smile,

I sought her even to the sagging board whereat

The stout immortals sat;

But such a laughter shook the mighty hall

No one could hear me say:

Had she been seen upon the Hill that day?

And no one knew at all

How long I stood, or when at last I sighed and

 went away.

There is a garden lying in a lull

Between the mountains and the mountainous sea,

I know not where, but which a dream diurnal

Paints on my lids a moment till the hull

Be lifted from the kernel

And Slumber fed to me.

Your foot-print is not there, Mnemosene,

Though it would seem a ruined place and after

ODE TO SILENCE

Your lichenous heart, being full

Of broken columns, caryatides

Thrown to the earth and fallen forward on their

    jointless knees,

And urns funereal altered into dust

Minuter than the ashes of the dead,

And Psyche's lamp out of the earth up-thrust,

Dripping itself in marble wax on what was once

    the bed

Of Love, and his young body asleep, but now is

    dust instead.

There twists the bitter-sweet, the white wisteria

Fastens its fingers in the strangling wall,

And the wide crannies quicken with bright

    weeds;

There dumbly like a worm all day the still white
    orchid feeds;
But never an echo of your daughters' laughter
Is there, nor any sign of you at all
Swells fungous from the rotten bough, grey mother
    of Pieria!

Only her shadow once upon a stone
I saw,—and, lo, the shadow and the garden, too,
    were gone.

I tell you you have done her body an ill,
You chatterers, you noisy crew!
She is not anywhere!
I sought her in deep Hell;
And through the world as well;
I thought of Heaven and I sought her there;

ODE TO SILENCE

Above nor under ground

Is Silence to be found,

That was the very warp and woof of you,

Lovely before your songs began and after they

    were through!

Oh, say if on this hill

Somewhere your sister's body lies in death,

So I may follow there, and make a wreath

Of my locked hands, that on her quiet breast

Shall lie till age has withered them!

                    (Ah, sweetly from the rest

I see

Turn and consider me

Compassionate Euterpe!)

"There is a gate beyond the gate of Death,

Beyond the gate of everlasting Life,

Beyond the gates of Heaven and Hell," she
saith,

"Whereon but to believe is horror!

Whereon to meditate engendereth

Even in deathless spirits such as I

A tumult in the breath,

A chilling of the inexhaustible blood

Even in my veins that never will be dry,

And in the austere, divine monotony

That is my being, the madness of an unaccustomed
mood.

This is her province whom you lack and seek;

And seek her not elsewhere.

Hell is a thoroughfare

For pilgrims,—Herakles,

And he that loved Euridice too well,

Have walked therein; and many more than these;

And witnessed the desire and the despair

Of souls that passed reluctantly and sicken for the

    air;

You, too, have entered Hell,

And issued thence; but thence whereof I speak

None has returned;—for thither fury brings

Only the driven ghosts of them that flee before all

    things.

Oblivion is the name of this abode: and she is

    there."

Oh, radiant Song! Oh, gracious Memory!

Be long upon this height

I shall not climb again!

I know the way you mean,—the little night,

And the long empty day,—never to see

Again the angry light,

Or hear the hungry noises cry my brain!

Ah, but she,

Your other sister and my other soul,

She shall again be mine;

And I shall drink her from a silver bowl,

A chilly thin green wine,

Not bitter to the taste,

Not sweet,

Not of your press, oh, restless, clamorous nine,—

To foam beneath the frantic hoofs of mirth—

But savoring faintly of the acid earth,

And trod by pensive feet

From perfect clusters ripened without haste

Out of the urgent heat

In some clear glimmering vaulted twilight under
the odorous vine.

Lift up your lyres! Sing on!

But as for me, I seek your sister whither she is
gone.

MEMORIAL TO D. C.
[VASSAR COLLEGE, 1918]

Oh, loveliest throat of all sweet throats,

Where now no more the music is,

With hands that wrote you little notes

I write you little elegies!

EPITAPH

HEAP not on this mound
    Roses that she loved so well;
Why bewilder her with roses,
    That she cannot see or smell?
She is happy where she lies
With the dust upon her eyes.

PRAYER TO PERSEPHONE

Be to her, Persephone,

All the things I might not be;

Take her head upon your knee.

She that was so proud and wild,

Flippant, arrogant and free,

She that had no need of me,

Is a little lonely child

Lost in Hell,—Persephone,

Take her head upon your knee;

Say to her, "My dear, my dear,

It is not so dreadful here."

CHORUS

GIVE away her gowns,

Give away her shoes;

She has no more use

For her fragrant gowns;

Take them all down,

Blue, green, blue,

Lilac, pink, blue,

From their padded hangers;

She will dance no more

In her narrow shoes;

Sweep her narrow shoes

From the closet floor.

ELEGY

Let them bury your big eyes
In the secret earth securely,
Your thin fingers, and your fair,
Soft, indefinite-colored hair,—
All of these in some way, surely,
From the secret earth shall rise;
Not for these I sit and stare,
Broken and bereft completely;
Your young flesh that sat so neatly
On your little bones will sweetly
Blossom in the air.

But your voice,—never the rushing
Of a river underground,

Not the rising of the wind

In the trees before the rain,

Not the woodcock's watery call,

Not the note the white-throat utters,

Not the feet of children pushing

Yellow leaves along the gutters

In the blue and bitter fall,

Shall content my musing mind

For the beauty of that sound

That in no new way at all

Ever will be heard again.

Sweetly through the sappy stalk

Of the vigorous weed,

Holding all it held before,

Cherished by the faithful sun,

ELEGY

On and on eternally

Shall your altered fluid run,

Bud and bloom and go to seed;

But your singing days are done;

But the music of your talk

Never shall the chemistry

Of the secret earth restore.

All your lovely words are spoken.

Once the ivory box is broken,

Beats the golden bird no more.

DIRGE

Boys and girls that held her dear,
  Do your weeping now;
All you loved of her lies here.

Brought to earth the arrogant brow,
  And the withering tongue
Chastened; do your weeping now.

Sing whatever songs are sung,
  Wind whatever wreath,
For a playmate perished young,

For a spirit spent in death.
Boys and girls that held her dear,
All you loved of her lies here.

SONNETS

I

WE talk of taxes, and I call you friend;

Well, such you are,—but well enough we know

How thick about us root, how rankly grow

Those subtle weeds no man has need to tend,

That flourish through neglect, and soon must send

Perfume too sweet upon us and overthrow

Our steady senses; how such matters go

We are aware, and how such matters end.

Yet shall be told no meagre passion here;

With lovers such as we forevermore

Isolde drinks the draught, and Guinevere

Receives the Table's ruin through her door,

Francesca, with the loud surf at her ear,

Lets fall the colored book upon the floor.

II

Into the golden vessel of great song

Let us pour all our passion; breast to breast

Let other lovers lie, in love and rest;

Not we,—articulate, so, but with the tongue

Of all the world: the churning blood, the long

Shuddering quiet, the desperate hot palms pressed

Sharply together upon the escaping guest,

The common soul, unguarded, and grown strong.

Longing alone is singer to the lute;

Let still on nettles in the open sigh

The minstrel, that in slumber is as mute

As any man, and love be far and high,

That else forsakes the topmost branch, a fruit

Found on the ground by every passer-by.

III

Not with libations, but with shouts and laughter
We drenched the altars of Love's sacred grove,
Shaking to earth green fruits, impatient after
The launching of the colored moths of Love.
Love's proper myrtle and his mother's zone
We bound about our irreligious brows,
And fettered him with garlands of our own,
And spread a banquet in his frugal house.
Not yet the god has spoken; but I fear
Though we should break our bodies in his flame,
And pour our blood upon his altar, here
Henceforward is a grove without a name,
A pasture to the shaggy goats of Pan,
Whence flee forever a woman and a man.

IV

Only until this cigarette is ended,

A little moment at the end of all,

While on the floor the quiet ashes fall,

And in the firelight to a lance extended,

Bizarrely with the jazzing music blended,

The broken shadow dances on the wall,

I will permit my memory to recall

The vision of you, by all my dreams attended.

And then adieu,—farewell!—the dream is done.

Yours is a face of which I can forget

The color and the features, every one,

The words not ever, and the smiles not yet;

But in your day this moment is the sun

Upon a hill, after the sun has set.

V

Once more into my arid days like dew,

Like wind from an oasis, or the sound

Of cold sweet water bubbling underground,

A treacherous messenger, the thought of you

Comes to destroy me; once more I renew

Firm faith in your abundance, whom I found

Long since to be but just one other mound

Of sand, whereon no green thing ever grew.

And once again, and wiser in no wise,

I chase your colored phantom on the air,

And sob and curse and fall and weep and rise

And stumble pitifully on to where,

Miserable and lost, with stinging eyes,

Once more I clasp,—and there is nothing there.

VI

No rose that in a garden ever grew,

In Homer's or in Omar's or in mine,

Though buried under centuries of fine

Dead dust of roses, shut from sun and dew

Forever, and forever lost from view,

But must again in fragrance rich as wine

The grey aisles of the air incarnadine

When the old summers surge into a new.

Thus when I swear, "I love with all my heart,"

'Tis with the heart of Lilith that I swear,

'Tis with the love of Lesbia and Lucrece;

And thus as well my love must lose some part

Of what it is, had Helen been less fair,

Or perished young, or stayed at home in Greece.

VII

When I too long have looked upon your face,

Wherein for me a brightness unobscured

Save by the mists of brightness has its place,

And terrible beauty not to be endured,

I turn away reluctant from your light,

And stand irresolute, a mind undone,

A silly, dazzled thing deprived of sight

From having looked too long upon the sun.

Then is my daily life a narrow room

In which a little while, uncertainly,

Surrounded by impenetrable gloom,

Among familiar things grown strange to me

Making my way, I pause, and feel, and hark,

Till I become accustomed to the dark.

VIII

And you as well must die, belovèd dust,

And all your beauty stand you in no stead;

This flawless, vital hand, this perfect head,

This body of flame and steel, before the gust

Of Death, or under his autumnal frost,

Shall be as any leaf, be no less dead

Than the first leaf that fell,—this wonder fled.

Altered, estranged, disintegrated, lost.

Nor shall my love avail you in your hour.

In spite of all my love, you will arise

Upon that day and wander down the air

Obscurely as the unattended flower,

It mattering not how beautiful you were,

Or how belovèd above all else that dies.

Let you not say of me when I am old,

In pretty worship of my withered hands

Forgetting who I am, and how the sands

Of such a life as mine run red and gold

Even to the ultimate sifting dust, "Behold,

Here walketh passionless age!"—for there expands

A curious superstition in these lands,

And by its leave some weightless tales are told.

In me no lenten wicks watch out the night;

I am the booth where Folly holds her fair;

Impious no less in ruin than in strength,

When I lie crumbled to the earth at length,

Let you not say, "Upon this reverend site

The righteous groaned and beat their breasts in

    prayer."

X

Oh, my belovèd, have you thought of this:

How in the years to come unscrupulous Time,

More cruel than Death, will tear you from my kiss,

And make you old, and leave me in my prime?

How you and I, who scale together yet

A little while the sweet, immortal height

No pilgrim may remember or forget,

As sure as the world turns, some granite night

Shall lie awake and know the gracious flame

Gone out forever on the mutual stone;

And call to mind that on the day you came

I was a child, and you a hero grown?—

And the night pass, and the strange morning break

Upon our anguish for each other's sake!

As to some lovely temple, tenantless

Long since, that once was sweet with shivering

    brass,

Knowing well its altars ruined and the grass

Grown up between the stones, yet from excess

Of grief hard driven, or great loneliness,

The worshiper returns, and those who pass

Marvel him crying on a name that was,—

So is it now with me in my distress.

Your body was a temple to Delight;

Cold are its ashes whence the breath is fled,

Yet here one time your spirit was wont to move;

Here might I hope to find you day or night,

And here I come to look for you, my love,

Even now, foolishly, knowing you are dead.

XII

Cherish you then the hope I shall forget

At length, my lord, Pieria?—put away

For your so passing sake, this mouth of clay,

These mortal bones against my body set,

For all the puny fever and frail sweat

Of human love,—renounce for these, I say,

The Singing Mountain's memory, and betray

The silent lyre that hangs upon me yet?

Ah, but indeed, some day shall you awake,

Rather, from dreams of me, that at your side

So many nights, a lover and a bride,

But stern in my soul's chastity, have lain,

To walk the world forever for my sake,

And in each chamber find me gone again!

WILD SWANS

I looked in my heart while the wild swans went
    over.
And what did I see I had not seen before?
Only a question less or a question more;
Nothing to match the flight of wild birds flying.
Tiresome heart, forever living and dying,
House without air, I leave you and lock your door.
Wild swans, come over the town, come over
The town again, trailing your legs and crying!